THEY ONLY

SAW FEET

2007-8 NMI
MISSION EDUCATION RESOURCES

✵ ✵ ✵

BOOKS

AFRICA'S SOUL HOPE
The AIDS Crisis and the Church
by Ellen Decker

BABOONS ON THE RUNWAY
And Other Humorous Stories from Africa
by Richard F. Zanner

MEETING JESUS
by Keith Schwanz

THE NUDGE IN MY SIDE
Stories from Indonesia and the Philippines
by The Bob McCroskeys

THEY SAW ONLY FEET
More Life Lessons from Missionary Kids
by Dean Nelson

A LOVE STORY FROM TRINIDAD
by Ruth O. Saxon

✵ ✵ ✵

ADULT MISSION EDUCATION RESOURCE BOOK

RESPONDING TO MISSION CHALLENGES
Editors: Aimee Curtis and Rosanne Bolerjack

THEY ONLY SAW FEET

More Life Lessons from
Missionary Kids

by
DEAN NELSON

Nazarene Publishing House
Kansas City, Missouri

Copyright 2007
Nazarene Publishing House

ISBN-13: 978-0-8341-2290-1
ISBN-10: 0-8341-2290-1

Printed in the United States of America

Editor: Aimee Curtis
Cover Design: Chad Cherry
Interior Design: Sharon Page

10 9 8 7 6 5 4 3 2 1

DEDICATION

Dedicated to the memory of my grandparents,
Paul and Naomi Cunningham, who told the
story of Jesus wherever they went

CONTENTS

Dean Nelson is the director of the journalism program at Point Loma Nazarene University in San Diego. He has written for the *New York Times, Boston Globe, Christianity Today,* and several other national publications. He has won several awards from the Society of Professional Journalists. He is the author of 12 books, mostly on spiritual themes, including *Every Full Moon Night,* an NMI missions book for 2006-2007.

Dean has traveled throughout the world, covering stories of human interest: India, where he wrote about the slums of Bombay; Kosovo, where he interviewed and wrote about victims of terrorism; Africa, where he wrote about members of the Black Panther Party who live in exile; Dominican Republic, where he wrote about people drinking clean water; and New Orleans, where he wrote about survivors of Hurricane Katrina.

He has a doctorate in journalism from Ohio University in Athens, Ohio; a master's degree in journalism from the University of Missouri at Columbia; and a bachelor's degree from MidAmerica Nazarene University in Olathe, Kansas.

Dr. Nelson grew up in Minnesota and, he admits, "I'm a die-hard hockey player and fan." He is married to his college sweetheart, Marcia, and they have a son, Blake, and a daughter, Vanessa.

FOREWORD

We live in a rapid world that rewards impatience and short-term thinking. Companies are valued by how they performed in the past three months, and how they project they will perform in the next three months. Because of how modern electronics have shaped our lives, we tend to get impatient when we have to wait for anything. Waiting on a computer or a cell phone, for instance, drives us crazy if it takes more than a few seconds.

But that's not how God works. The Lord's timing is completely different from ours. When we respond to God's call, we want and often expect instant results. The truth is, however, that we may not see the immediate fruit of our labor. That's what the life of a missionary is—responding to God's call in God's time. A missionary is a person on a mission. A missionary is a person who carries the gospel across cultural, language, and ethnic barriers.

Many missionaries have served in settings where people were resistant or even antagonistic to the gospel. In those settings, Kingdom missionaries patiently become Christ incarnate to those persons, carefully planting the gospel seed in their hearts and lives. Other missionaries have served in settings where God's prevenient grace used the faithful witness of earlier believers to prepare a precious harvest. My parents served in Puerto Rico, New Zealand, Venezuela, and Spain. The level of fruitfulness varied significantly from place to place, but in all these assignments they were true to their call. In our fast-paced world we want instant results and instant gratification. We are wise, however, when we embrace the perspective of the eternal Kingdom that is like a seed that dies and then springs to life in the Lord's time.

That's what this book is about. I identified with many of the stories, having grown up as a missionary kid and served as a missionary. We know about making sacrifices, expecting miracles, praying for protection, seeing the strong role that women play in ministry, praying for hours, dealing with conflict, embracing a new culture, confronting evil spirits, and celebrating the precious eternal fruit to the glory of God. My wife and I could also identify with those who followed God, despite what they were feeling and despite the short-term discouragements. These missionaries followed God for the long-term. They are great role models for all of us.

Any success I had in fulfilling God's call on me as a missionary had a great deal to do with the missionaries and Christian servants who served before me. I truly felt that I was standing on the shoulders of giants like those in this book.

But you don't have to be a missionary to appreciate this book. You just need to be a person who believes God still calls people to serve as partners on a divine mission. We live in a short-term, nearsighted culture, but we serve an eternal, timeless God.

Jerry Porter
General Superintendent,
Church of the Nazarene

INTRODUCTION

This is the second of two volumes that came out of a series of discussions and interviews I conducted with several adults who grew up in countries outside the United States as their parents or grandparents served God as missionaries. Sometimes their families were part of new works, where there had not been a Christian or Nazarene presence in a region before. Other times they were part of missionary work that had been started generations before them, and they continued the task of sharing the Good News.

Each missionary kid expressed a similar theme, though. They watched their parents, and sometimes grandparents, do what few of us could do today, in my opinion. They watched them withstand hardship, personal and emotional pain, doubt, rejection, fear, and distance from loved ones, then turn it into joy, peace, longsuffering, humility, patience, and victory. Entire nations are reaping the benefit of having people in their governments and other leadership positions who are believers in Jesus Christ, thanks to the work of Nazarene missionaries in those countries generations ago.

The first volume of these accounts was published in 2006 under the title *Every Full Moon Night: Life Lessons from Missionary Kids*. That title came from the story told by Jo Cunningham and Kiddy Sullivan about their father, Everette Howard, who would pray all night and read Scripture by the light of the moon for the people of the Cape Verde Islands. The title of this volume comes from the story told by Anita Birchard Reglin about her grandparents preaching in Guatemala to an empty church. They held services in that church for a solid year with not one person coming inside. But her grandparents knew the people of the village were listening because they could see their feet outside the church walls. Eventually people began coming inside.

When times got difficult for some of the missionaries in this book, they often wondered if they had misinterpreted the call that they felt God had placed on their minds and hearts. "If God wants us here, then why are things going so badly?" was a legitimate question, and one that I think most of us understand. We have this notion of God that, if we believe we are following Him, things will go smoothly. That notion is not supported in Scripture, and it is not supported in real life or in the accounts of these missionaries. What I think is remarkable is what the missionaries did *after* they asked that question. They kept going despite the evidence, then watched the evidence change.

Here's why: they trusted God above everything else. They trusted the call from God and its authenticity. That meant they didn't have to trust the evidence around them. Can you imagine preaching to an empty church for a solid year? What kind of evidence or assurance is that? But that's not how Anita's grandparents measured their efforts. They measured them by asking, "Are we doing what God called us to do?" The results take care of themselves.

So even though this is a collection of stories and experiences from years ago, I believe they have application to our lives today. It's good denominational history. But it's more than that. It's an example of how God has worked through history, and how He still works today if we truly follow Him.

Special thanks to Ray Hendrix and Franklin Cook for their dream to see these accounts be shared throughout the denomination, and to Pat Braselton of World Mission Literature for her help in getting the pieces of this project to fit, as well as to Premier Studios in Lenexa, Kansas, for providing us their space and equipment for our discussions.

Thanks also to the missionary kids and grandkids who continue to bear witness to the work of God around the world.

And thanks especially to God, who continues to call, to challenge, to stretch, to use people like those in this book—and us—to reach the world that it may be brought back into right relationship with Him.

Dean Nelson

San Diego, California

1 THEY SAW ONLY FEET

by Anita Birchard Reglin

Anita Birchard Reglin's grandfather, Richard Simpson Anderson, helped pioneer missionary work in Guatemala in 1904. Her parents, Russell and Margaret Birchard, served as missionaries in Guatemala for 29 years and in Nicaragua for 10 years. Anita was born in Guatemala.

When my grandfather was a teenager living in South Carolina, a revival meeting came to the area. The travelers set up a tent in the middle of town. My grandfather's curiosity got the better of him, so he went in to see what was happening. He was saved and sanctified in that meeting. Shortly after that he went to a Bible college and met Maude Watson, who became his wife. While they were in Bible studies there, talking about mission work, they both accepted a call from God to become missionaries. This was in 1903, well before the Church of the Nazarene started sending missionaries.

They took a ship to Guatemala. They didn't know anyone, and they didn't even know the language. So they spent several months in a town teaching English and trying to get acquainted. That was a very traumatic and difficult time for them. They finally made some contacts in a different town and moved there to learn Spanish. But while they were there, yellow fever broke out and the epidemic ravaged the city. More than 500 people died in that village. They were dying so fast that the bodies were loaded onto an ox cart during the night to be taken away in the morning.

My grandparents both contracted the disease. They were living by themselves and had no help. They were not even well enough to get food. But a neighbor—a Catholic lady—looked in on them and discovered them in this terrible state. She made soup and nursed them back to health.

Did We Misinterpret Something?

On top of all of this, my grandparents ran out of money. They had not yet learned the language, they were nearly dying, and they battled with whether the Lord had really directed them to Guatemala. Had they misinterpreted something? I think we have all been in places where we have wondered if we misinterpreted the leading of God.

They survived, started a new mission work in a different area, and stayed there for 40 years.

The call from God they received in their late teens and early 20s in Bible school was what they clung to. It was an unwavering commitment, even though they wondered about it during those early days. Even in this new region they had reason to question whether God had really led them there. Because of the heavy Catholic influence in the area, people were afraid to go inside my grandparents' little Protestant church. They were afraid of being ridiculed, of losing their businesses, of physical abuse, and worse. They didn't want to be seen associating with Protestants. So for a solid year, my grandmother played the organ and my grandfather preached to a completely empty building. Not one person came inside. For a year!

But my grandparents knew the people in the area were listening because there was a space below the wooden walls and above the ground where they could see feet. All this time the people were standing around the outside of the walls listening, hearing the gospel. Then, finally, some soul had the courage to step inside and accept the Lord. That was the beginning. But it began by singing and preaching to an empty building. My grandparents didn't question whether or not the message was "working." They didn't count whether or not the church was full. They simply clung to their call.

A Privilege, Not a Hardship

During the week, my grandmother's approach to sharing Jesus was subtle. She had some large rock-

Margaret Birchard

Russell Birchard

ing chairs on her porch, and people would line up waiting to come rock with her. They would talk, and she would listen and counsel and help and pray. She had a great work that wasn't always visible.

My mother went to the United States for her education, where she met my father. They decided that they, too, were being directed by God to Guatemala as missionaries. But a lot changed in the years my mother was gone. Guatemala became a Communist country, and a new regulation prohibited the arrival of new missionaries. The government refused to give permission to my parents to come to Guatemala. When the town where they were headed heard they were planning to come, but the government wasn't permitting them, leaders in the community started a petition. Since my mother was a nurse, the town petitioned to let her in because the town needed the medical help. So the government allowed my parents to come. Many times my mother worked at the medical clinic, and my father helped her and preached to the people in the waiting room.

My parents always viewed what they did as an absolute privilege. Their attitude was the key to our comfort. We were not aware of their sacrifices or difficulties at the time. We were raised with the sense that it was always a privilege to be a missionary's child.

We did not have to go to boarding school; we had a one-room building in our village that served six grades. For the upper grades we went to another town, but it was where our grandmother lived, so we stayed with her.

I have wonderful memories of where I grew up. I still got teary-eyed when I hear the national anthem of Guatemala.

I was very happy living in Guatemala and didn't want to leave when it was time to go to school in the United States. I figured that I wouldn't have to go if I would just flunk something. So I purposely flunked math. They sent me anyway.

The Birchard family sets sail for Guatemala, 1941
(Anita is standing in the back).

My parents did a good job of helping us love both Guatemala and the United States. I have wonderful memories of where I grew up. I still get teary-eyed when I hear the national anthem of Guatemala. That is my home country.

We had a family worship time every day. If my father was on the road, my mother took charge of it. It wasn't rushed, because we didn't go anywhere very fast. It was always in Spanish because there would always be someone helping, either a cook or someone helping in the yard. We wanted to make sure they heard what God had been doing—it was always pleasant. As kids we did not object to it. When we all left to go away to school, we knew that every day we were being prayed for by name and that our parents had tremendous confidence in us.

My parents' greatest joy was in bonding with the people of their community. My mother was born in Guatemala, so she knew the culture and the language. My father learned it quickly. They dearly loved the people there. When they came to the United States on furlough, they could hardly wait to get back. They were going home when they went back to the mission field.

Provision and Protection

As missionaries, we came to expect miracles. One day we were traveling in our truck—five children and our parents—during heavy rains, and it began to flood. It wasn't unusual for the floods to be so bad that they came to the rooftops of the homes. We were driving along and came to a bridge across a river. It just had planks across it and no sides. The water was just above the bridge. My dad looked it over, and he and Mother debated whether to proceed or to wait. Dad decided it was safe to go on. You could not see the bridge, but you could see where it should be. Now that's faith. We started across and got into the middle of this long bridge. Apparently there were some planks out, though, because the front tires went down. We were absolutely stuck in the car, with the water rising.

We prayed and prayed and prayed, because we knew that the next step was for the water to rise so much that it would take our truck down the river. We stayed on the bridge, praying, and the water began to recede. Soon after the water receded, passers-by came along and lifted the truck out of the hole. We were able to proceed. Events like that will stay in my mind forever, and I have come to expect that God will protect and provide.

We had a lot of sickness in our part of the country, and my parents went to great lengths to keep us healthy. They boiled and filtered the water, didn't let us go barefoot, did everything they could. But they must have wondered how we still got sick when they were protecting us so much. It's because we kept doing things we weren't supposed to do.

For example, my sister and I went to piano lessons on the other side of town. To get there, we had to go through the bazaar—the big market. Just inside the market was a lady who sold these wonderful drinks. She would slice pineapple, peaches, and other fruit, and put them in a pan with the peelings on, not washed, and leave them in to ferment a little bit. Then she took the juice from the fruit to make this drink. It had a nice kick to it. We weren't supposed to touch anything like that, but we did. To wash the dishes, she simply rolled the glasses in a tub of water. The market didn't have running water;

this water had been brought in from who knows where. So she rolled the glasses in that water and then served them to the next customers.

Farther into the market was a lady who sold candy. It was a cross between taffy and caramel, and we loved it. She put some in a banana leaf for us, and we ate it on the way to the piano lesson. One day, as we made our way through this crowded market, we got to the candy lady's booth and saw that she was sitting on the dirt floor with both legs out, her skirt pulled up as far as it would go. She rolled the candy on her bare legs. We were smart enough to know we wouldn't be eating that candy any more.

Fear, Grief, and Yet . . .

People sent us things from the United States, but the government charged a duty on anything that came in. One time a big box came for us, and my dad sensed that it was important, so he cashed in his trumpet to pay the duty. It turned out to be a fur coat. In Guatemala.

In the 1950s, when the communists took over the government of Guatemala, a number of pastors were arrested and executed. They sent two soldiers to our address and gave orders to arrest the man of the house. When the soldiers got there, they said there must be a mistake. The government couldn't have meant to arrest *him,* they said. These soldiers had attended my father's church. They couldn't imagine arresting him. So they didn't. We were able to survive that frightening time, but again, my parents believed God had placed them there and would guide, direct, and protect them.

The few times my parents were upset were when they received sad news from family. It was difficult back then to travel to and from the United States, even though it wasn't that far in actual miles. My father's brother and mother both died while he was in Guatemala. As I've read through my parents' letters, I've learned that this was an extremely grievous time for them. They weren't able to go back for the funerals or to be with their families. All they could do was respond through letters.

Occasionally they had problems within the church structure too. Because of timing and specific circumstances, sometimes responsibilities were given to missionaries who did not have the personalities to match the tasks. My father became a district superintendent (D.S.) in Guatemala because the former D.S. had become ill and had to leave. But my father did not have the personality for that kind of administrative job. He was not good at delegating. His strong personality rubbed against some of the younger missionaries who had different ideas of how

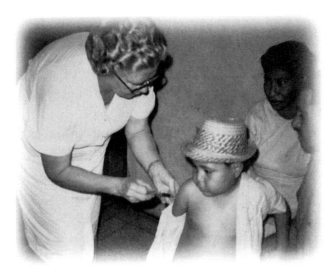

Anita's mother ministering in Nicaragua

things should be done. So after 29 years of serving in Guatemala, my parents were voted off the field by the local missionary council.

The good news is that God can be glorified in everything. They went on to have 10 of the most rewarding years of their lives in Nicaragua. I don't think they would trade their experience those last 10 years for anything, even though it was painful to experience rejection in Guatemala. The Lord worked it out.

Much has changed since my grandparents went

to Guatemala, with no institution behind them, without knowing the language, and without a specific assignment. What hasn't changed is that people still need to hear the gospel and that God still calls some to leave their homes to spread that Good News in places far away. The call on people's hearts today is every bit as real as it was when God called my grandparents.

So I tell people considering going into missions that they should go all out and give it everything they can. They should assume they are going for life. They should make the mission field the real home for their children—not just a temporary place. They should focus on the people and the culture, and leave everything else behind. It's like going into a marriage contract. You can't go in with the idea that "If it works, fine; if it doesn't, I'll do something else."

If that had been the case with my grandparents, they would have left after experiencing fever. They would have given up after a year with no one coming in their church. But they persevered. They clung to their call. That call was bigger than the results. And people know Jesus throughout Central America because my grandparents trusted God more than anything else.

Forty years after my grandfather died, the government of Guatemala named a public school after him. I thought that decision was made by the local school council where he had served for so long. But then I found out the decision was made at the national level. Many of the boys and girls he taught are now in positions of leadership in the government, and they wanted to honor him.

We all must keep our faith in the One who calls us. You just never know whose feet you might be preaching to.

2 THAT COULD BE US

by John Anderson

John Anderson's parents, John and Mary Anderson, served as missionaries in India from 1936 to 1970. The younger John Anderson and his wife, Doris, also served in India from 1966 to 1998.

The concept of holiness caused my grandparents more grief than anyone could imagine. First of all, it got them kicked out of the Lutheran church. They went over to the Methodist church after that, but when they heard the Methodist bishop call John Wesley a fool, they knew it was time to move on again. The result was that they started their own church—a Church of the Nazarene. They became pioneer Nazarenes in both Ohio and Pennsylvania.

My grandfather was a Swedish carpenter who came to America by himself at the tender age of 14. He didn't know much English, and he didn't care for anything literary, but he learned a great deal of English from reading his Bible. He also read John Wesley's *A Plain Account of Christian Perfection.* Here he was, an uneducated carpenter who really only wanted a church that preached this kind of message. In the written record of my grandparents' old Lutheran church it says, in Swedish, and in not very nice language, that my grandfather was kicked out for talking about holiness and sanctification. Then it continues for several more unkind words about him. That's when they began attending a Methodist church—that is until the bishop called Wesley a fool.

About that time, a holiness revival sponsored by The Salvation Army came to town. This was around 1905 or so. Close to eight or nine families who attended the revival decided to form a holiness group. They mortgaged their houses and bought a block of land where they established the Church of the Nazarene. A year or so later, the Pittsburgh District of the Church of the Nazarene formed, and my grandfather's church joined that district.

"Did You Read *The Other Sheep?*"

My father was not called into the ministry at first. He went to Eastern Nazarene College, got an education degree, taught math, and played piano for local music groups. When he sensed a call from God to be a missionary, he went to Boston University for a master's degree in theology. He almost married a woman who was called to be a missionary to India and whose parents were missionaries in India. But he didn't want any part of that, so they broke up. Because he was involved in music—even playing for a summer with the Boston Pops—he was afraid if he went someplace as remote as India, he would not be able to keep his music interests going.

When he married my mother, she was already ordained and had started churches in Maine. She was an excellent preacher, better than my father. Together they planted churches in West Virginia and Ohio. When I was about three, they became missionaries to India. I know what you're thinking. He broke up with a woman who wanted to be a missionary to India because that's not what he wanted to do. Then he married someone else and they became missionaries to India. How does something like this happen? Let me tell you. Nazarene Publishing House used to print a missions publication called *The Other Sheep.* My parents read it regularly as part of their devotions. One month an announcement in the magazine read, "We need a missionary couple for India." My mother saw it and said to herself, "That could be us, but I don't know about *him.*" And my father saw it and said, "That could be us, but I don't know about *her.*" They each prayed about what they sensed was the leading of God.

The next morning at breakfast, a dialogue happened like this:

"Did you read *The Other Sheep?*"

"Yes."

"Did you read the article about needing missionaries in India?"

The Other Sheep

"Yes."

"Well, what do you think?"

"Let's go!"

Not much later they drove their Model A Ford to the Nazarene general assembly in St. Louis—with several flat tires along the way—and were appointed missionaries to Central India. Dad did not have to give up his music.

Boarding School Life

My parents sent me to boarding school when I was five or six years old. I don't recall it being a difficult time for me, but it was hard for my mom and dad. Later, when I sent my own two children, I understood how my parents must have felt.

During the time I was in school, India was experiencing a great amount of turmoil. Fights often broke out in the popular gathering areas, mostly over religious or political beliefs. One Saturday afternoon my friends and I happened to be in the central bazaar when a riot broke out. We took off running back to the school, and life went on as if nothing had happened. These kinds of things occurred frequently. It was treated as just another fight in the bazaar.

Boarding school was an enriching time for me. I attended with missionary kids from other churches, as well as Hindus, Muslims, and others—some of whom are now highly placed in the Indian government. In fact, when I traveled to India recently, I had ready access to the prime minister because he was my former classmate. Another classmate of mine was a relative of the Shah of Iran. He taught me Arabic. I was able to use that language skill when I retired and worked with Arab groups in the United States.

Even though I was far away from home—a 48-hour train ride—I look at my boarding school experience as a blessing. At times it was simply hilarious. For example, I remember throwing a rock at one of the monkeys that lived near my school. Only he caught it and threw it back at me. It scared me half to death! I ran for my life. Another time several of us students had the chicken pox. We were all lying in bed, bored to tears, when a large monkey appeared in the doorway. We egged him on and made faces at him. He imitated everything we did. Finally he marched into our room and discovered the dresser with the mirror above it. He got up on the dresser and looked at himself, made some faces at the reflection, then made a fist and held it out. He didn't like what he saw, so he smashed his fist into the mirror—which, amazingly, did not break. He hit it several more times. Soon a friend of his came in, and they got into a fight on the dresser. This was wonderful for us to watch—better than television. We clapped and had a great time. It was the best entertainment we had seen in weeks.

For the seemingly endless train ride home, my friends and I climbed up on the engine and shoveled coal to help produce steam. We all had slingshots, too, and would pick crows off the telegraph line.

Life in India was full of surprises. Once my father and I went to a town for a business meeting about 40 miles away. When we came back, it was dark. There were no lights anywhere except for the headlights on our car. We came around a curve and saw a tiger lying across the road. We couldn't get around him. On one side of the road was a large drop. On the other was a steep hill. He was much bigger than us. In any battle, he would win. So we just sat there for a while. I asked my dad, "What are you going to do?" He said, "I don't know." He revved the engine a little, and the tiger looked at us with an expression that seemed to say, "Is there something bothering you?" We backed up a bit, but the tiger simply got up, stretched, and laid back down again. After a while, he finally stood up and walked back into the jungle. We were on our way at last.

A serious clash of cultures existed in India. Since that country was the crown jewel of the British Empire, some parts were very British. But other parts were very Indian. As Americans, we had to be somewhat three-dimensional in our thinking. For instance, if we wanted to get anything accomplished regarding property or registration, it was necessary to have good contacts with local officials. So my mother frequently had them over for tea. It was something she learned from Franklin Cook's mother. If you didn't have these connections, your hands were tied.

Her actions paid off later when my wife and I came back as missionaries. The kids I used to play with in the town were now the leaders in business, government, and in the churches. We had an instant rapport with almost everyone because these contacts had been made long ago.

In India, men appear to be the ones doing the majority of the work, but they always check with the women first. In Hinduism, the woman tends the shrine at home and takes the food to the idol in the village. It's a society where the men are visible and seemingly dominant, but in reality they're not. In the Church of the Nazarene, women do much of the work as well. Thankfully, our denomination has a heritage of women serving in leadership roles in the church.

When a Curse Becomes a Blessing

Still, not everyone welcomed the Christian message in India. One day I went to preach at a church that was having a difficult time dealing with harassment from the Hindus. I arrived a little early, and the pastor's family that was hosting me was not quite ready for my visit. His wife was in the middle of putting a fresh covering on the walls of their home. In Indian homes they take manure, mud, and water and mix it together to spread on the wall. Everything is fresh. She had her hands in the mixing bucket when I came in. We said good morning, and she finished her task. Then she washed her hands and brought tea. As we sat with our tea, the pastor introduced me to a new Christian, a pharmacist who worked in the local government hospital. He was excited to talk about his new faith, and we were excited with him about the way God was working in his life.

When we walked outside to go to the church, the pharmacist's wife approached him screaming. She took the Bible out of her husband's hand and stomped on it, embarrassing him greatly. This attracted a crowd of a couple hundred people. It was an effective means for gathering a good congregation for the services, though, because most of them came to the church to hear me

When I neared the culvert, a man appeared out of nowhere and put his hands up. "Don't go over," he said. "The bridge is out."

speak, wondering what I would say about this incident. I spoke from Isaiah, about how God knows your name. The pharmacist said to me after the service, "God knows my name—I'll never give up on that." Everyone in his family eventually became Christians, and his daughters are nurses in our hospital. The Lord also used that experience to bring 25 new members into the church.

On the trip home, I had to go across a dusty area for about three miles to get to the main road. I knew that soon after I got to the road there was a deep culvert, but I couldn't quite see it coming. When I neared it, though, a man appeared out of nowhere and put his hands up. "Don't go over," he said. "The bridge is out."

"How do you know?" I asked.

He simply replied, "Go around and below it."

I turned and went below it, and when I looked back, the man wasn't there. I think God sent an angel to warn me.

India is a place where people worship many different kinds of spirits. We rented a beautiful house with marble floors, but something about it didn't seem right. We just had a sense of something being out of sorts. Eventually we found an idol to the goddess of evil in the back of the house. I went to the owner of the property and said, "We need to have this taken out." But he simply moved it to another part of the house and nothing changed until I found it again. While I was out one day, my wife had someone help her take it to where they burn the trash, and they destroyed it. At about the same time I was on my motorcycle, and while they were destroying the idol, I had five near-accidents, one right after the other. I got home and told my wife how hard a time I had getting home. She told me that it was at the same time they were crushing the statue. Those spirits are real.

Likewise, though, since it is an Eastern culture, they have an easy time understanding the Bible. I have been able to give the Gospel of John to educated Hindus, and they see the plan of salvation simply by reading it. I don't have to say anything. The theology is understood immediately because of its Eastern cultural dimension.

Full Circle

My parents eventually retired and moved back to the United States. They visited Maine, and my mother preached in the church she had started. When they went to sleep that night, my mother woke up in heaven. My father didn't even know it until morning.

He also didn't know how to reach us because we had gone on a short vacation into the mountains of India. By the time we got back to Delhi, she had already been buried. It was traumatic. That's where the physical distance of being far away from loved ones is so difficult.

While in India, we received some interesting things from what I assume were well-meaning people in the United States. For example, someone sent us a 10-pound ham in the mail—without refrigeration. It took three or four months to get to us. By the time it reached our city, it smelled so bad they closed down the post office. A month later another one came, and the boy delivering it on his bicycle had to hold it as far away from his body as possible. I don't know what the people sending these things were thinking. We just chose to believe that anyone who sent us ham thousands of miles away, which took months to deliver, had good intentions. Maybe *The Other Sheep* had announced, "Missionaries in India need ham."

Thirty years after coming to India, I got up one morning to pray and it hit me that I had done what I came here to do. I was finished—I didn't need to stay any longer. Unknown to me, my wife in the next room was having the same experience at the same time. It was just like my parents' experience reading *The Other Sheep* when they sensed God leading them to India. We sensed that we had done all God expected of us, and we were free to move on. It was a very different feeling of satisfaction. It had never occurred to me that this was part of the call from God too.

I am now back where my grandfather started attending the Church of the Nazarene in 1908, happy for the heritage of my grandparents, who discovered the holiness message for our family, and for my parents who showed us the joy in following the call of God. They took risks and faced rejection in obeying what they sensed was direction from God. They sacrificed and went out on a limb for this call, only to discover that their interests matched completely what God was calling them into in India. My parents and grandparents were all the evidence I needed about the way God leads.

3 BACK TO THE ROCK

by Ted Esselstyn

Ted Esselstyn was born in Swaziland and grew up in southern Africa with his parents, William and Margaret Esselstyn, who became missionaries in 1928. Margaret died on the mission field, as did Ted's brother. Ted came back to the United States for college in the 1950s and returned as a missionary in 1968. More than half of his assignment involved developing schools, and he was the regional education coordinator for all of Africa.

My dad grew up in a Presbyterian church in Michigan. His uncle was a Presbyterian missionary in Iran —he's buried there—and had a great deal of influence in my dad's life. Even at a very young age my dad felt that God wanted him in some kind of ministry—not specifically missionary service, but something.

When Dad met my mom, a girl from a family that had been kicked out of the Methodist church for professing holiness, she was very sickly. She had to drop out of high school at one point because of illness. During that time she felt God calling her to be a missionary. She told the Lord, "I'm not well enough to be a missionary. You can't possibly be calling me." But the Lord made it very clear to her that if she responded to a call to the mission field, she would find herself well enough to go. So she went back to high school, finished, and went on to become a nurse. That's when her association with Dad began. She was not at all interested in getting married because she knew she was headed toward the mission field, and my dad did not have the same kind of call. His call was for some kind of Christian service, as far as he knew, but it was vague.

Mom gave him some early books on holiness, and he became convinced that this was the way Christians should live. Then he went to a revival where Uncle Buddy Robinson was the preacher. That influenced him greatly. He attended Eastern Nazarene College (ENC), and after Mom finished her nurse's training, she also went to ENC. She received additional training in midwifery because she figured she would need that on the mission field. It was a good thing she did because in the British structure in Africa, midwifery is standard practice. You can't get a license unless you can do midwifery.

Dad went on to get his master's degree at Boston University, and his courtship with Mom continued. I have the letters they wrote to each other. During the last year they wrote each other every day. Much of the content had to do with their spiritual growth and their commitment to God, God's desire for their lives, and God's way. Shortly after, they married and were commissioned as missionaries to Africa.

Dad's introduction to the work there was to build a coffin for Harmon Schmelzenbach Sr., who had been very ill. After Harmon died, my dad would go up to the place where Harmon used to pray and commit himself to carrying on the work Harmon had started. The depth of Harmon's commitment was contagious, and it influenced many lives.

That place of prayer was a rock on a hill above the mission station. Both Harmon and my dad went there frequently to recommit their lives and work to God. There was an Old Testament feel to much of the early missionary efforts. Just like the prophets of old, God told them to do difficult things. But that quality of obedience to God, that commitment, was very much a part of their lives. Nothing counted more for them than to be and do what God wanted them to do. I saw that in many people, and I especially saw it in my parents.

The World's Strongest Woman

During the World War II years and right after, the work of the Church of the Nazarene in Africa faced difficult times. The number of missionaries had dwindled, and many felt they had been working for too long in a small area when so many others needed to hear the gospel. As a result, churches held an around-the-clock prayer time. The first week of every month, 24 hours a day, various churches took a 3-hour block of time to pray. They wanted to be able to reach what was known as the colored race as well as the blacks. They wanted to go into cities and into new areas where no one had preached. They wanted to double the number of missionaries and bring back those who had left during the war.

For a while there were only two men on the entire Africa field. That meant there were many women running the mission stations, doing everything that needed to be done. Some of them were very intimidating in the power they had.

I'll never forget one woman in particular—the strongest person I had ever met. I was with her and some others on a trip when we had a flat tire. We were driving what looked like an old-fashioned sport-utility vehicle. The jack didn't work, so she had us take all of the lug nuts off the tire except one. When it was time to take off the last one, she put her back to the car and lifted it up while we pulled off the flat and put on the new tire. We were all very cautious with her after that.

In 1945 the floodgates opened, and we ended up with more than triple the number of missionaries we previously had. But while more missionaries came, we had no additional money for their housing. Sometimes as many as three families lived in one

Ted and Joan Esselstyn

house. This was probably one of the greatest tests of our sanctification. We had an acceleration of problems because everyone was trying to learn the language and their new roles all in very close quarters.

Things began to ease in 1949 when mission stations expanded and houses were built. But it was, in my opinion, one of the most difficult, pressure-filled times on the Africa field.

We sent our children to boarding school when they were about six years old. Our oldest daughter, Karen, became a mother of sorts to all the other missionary kids. The worst experiences were with the children who had been told by their parents that it was a terrible thing to have to go to boarding school. But those who went with the sense that it was an adventure didn't have nearly the difficulty. Our middle daughter insisted on going back to school, even when the others were sick. She didn't want to miss it. She was in second grade.

Creative Baptism

It was obvious to me that my parents valued bringing people to Christ and seeing them get educated. That's what they talked about most. Another thing that brought them pleasure was when a missionary succeeded. My dad used to say to the other missionaries, "Your first responsibility is to help your fellow missionary succeed. It's as we all succeed that we do what the Lord wants done." And this became the thrust. It gave him real joy when he saw it happen.

Missionaries by nature are flexible and resourceful. In northern Mozambique, after their war of independence from the Portuguese, several of us visited a church that normally ran about 40 to 50 people. I had just graduated from high school and was the driver. Five of us were in a 1952 Chevy fitted with tractor tires because of the rough country and bad roads. It took 13 hours to go the final 90 miles. When we finally arrived, the church members told us they wanted to have a baby dedication. When word got out in the village that we were going to dedicate babies, the number went from the 15 or so we were expecting to close to 150. Even the nonbelievers wanted to make sure they covered all the bases.

We came up with a good plan. My dad had one line to dedicate, another missionary had another, and the African pastor had another. Since the British influence was still strong, we used the British method of sprinkling water over the baby and then praying. This was challenging, though, because of all the things to hold at the same time: the baby, the manual to read from, and the water. Dad called up my mother, and she first held the manual and the baby, then she held the water while Dad dipped his fingers in it, prayed the prayer, and baptized the child. The other missionary did the same, and there was no problem.

The African pastor couldn't get his wife to help him, however. He was absolutely stuck. He had a baby, a manual, and the water. He looked at the other two, watched how effortlessly they were working, and considered his own dilemma. Then we could see a light go on in his mind. He put the water in his mouth and spit it on the baby's head. My mother nearly dropped everything.

That part of Mozambique was a very difficult area for us. Our mission effort had been there for 30 years, but we saw no real progress. The people were deeply committed, but not much was happening there. After the war, however, we went back and built a bigger church. More than 700 people jammed in. The overflow crowd outside the church even got angry when the ushers didn't come outside to collect the offering—they wanted to contribute. Several districts quickly developed. What had happened? A sociological change had occurred in the country after the war that made it possible for us to expand. But it wouldn't have happened if we hadn't already had a foundation there before the war. The sociological change opened the door, but it was important that we were already in place. Then when the harvest was ready, we moved in. That was an important lesson for all of us and probably still applies today.

God Will Provide

When I was growing up the housing was primitive. Once we had a general superintendent visit us, and when he returned to the United States he said that he had been in our house and it wasn't fit for pigs. My mother was horrified. He later apologized to her and said, "It had nothing to do with the way you kept your house, but we shouldn't have houses with mud floors and tin windows that hardly close. We shouldn't have houses like this for missionaries. That's what I was trying to say."

It didn't seem that bad to us growing up there, but we did carry Lysol with us wherever we went. At camp meetings, where everyone washed their dishes in the same place, there were two basins. The first one was where you rinsed off your plate, but that basin soon became soup. The second basin was where you rinsed it again. We'd then wipe the plates off with Lysol and let them dry. Many times we were the only ones around the camp meeting without health problems.

It was clear that we weren't in the hands of the church; we were in the hands of God.

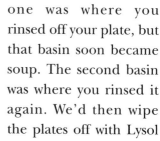

Years after my parents were gone, I read letters they sent back to the United States. I had no idea they were stretching so little into so much. It always seemed that we had plenty. For example, I didn't know we ate cornbread because we didn't have cake. To me, cornbread was great. One letter I read was from my mother to my dad when he was on one of his frequent trips away from home working as the field director. She wrote that in a few days we were going to have 23 people arriving and that they would be at our home over Christmas. She didn't know how she was going to feed everyone. Dad wrote back and said, "Don't worry about it. Get whatever you need to make it great. The Lord knows what you need, and the Lord will take care of you."

It was clear that we weren't in the hands of the church; we were in the hands of God, serving Him, doing His will. My parents' view was that He knew our needs, and it was our responsibility to do things properly. That's how we depended on God for everything.

Cultural Adjustments

Sometimes learning the language could be embarrassing. I once said at dinner what I thought was "I'm full," but in reality it meant "I'm pregnant" in Zulu. Another person we knew had a pink slip she wore under her dress. It was worn out, so she decided the best use for it was to stretch it over the barrel where they collected the drinking water from the roof of the house, for use as a cover. She thought she told a worker to "put it over the barrel," but she used the wrong word. She heard some noises outside and saw people struggling to put the slip on a donkey. It also shook her up when she tried to teach housekeeping skills to one of the girls working in the kitchen. She told the girl to go out and get the eggs from the chickens. The girl kept checking with her and asking, "Is that what you really want?" "Yes" was the impatient reply. But the word for "eggs" is close to the word for "heads" in that language, so our friend was not happy with what she got. We had a lot of chicken on the mission station after that.

Chicken heads are actually a delicacy. When I was a school principal, the children would beg us to buy bags of chicken heads and feet. You'd just throw them in a pot to boil, and the kids would line up with their hands out to get their boiled chicken heads, features and all. The kids would suck every last bit of flavor out of them. That made a good video for the start of a missionary training session.

Miracles That Transform

One of the biggest cultural differences my mother talked about was the African person's ability to deal with pain. She ran a health clinic as a nurse and was often called to a local hospital to help. She was amazed at how a patient would just stand there with an open mouth to have teeth pulled, with no anesthetic. One day she and Dr. Hynd were driving to the clinic, and a chief stopped them by the road-side and said that his hand was sore. They took the rags off it, and he had a gangrenous thumb. Dr. Hynd said it had to come off, so he told the chief to get in the car so they could take him to the clinic. The chief said he wasn't going anywhere and wanted them to do it right there.

The only thing they had in the car was a bandage and scissors. The chief stood there while they took the thumb off with the scissors and then bandaged him up. He never even whimpered. It needed to come off, and he dealt with it.

Many times things happened that couldn't be anything other than God at work. On one long car trip that involved about 200 miles of driving over sand, our car battery died. We had to take the battery out, connect the terminals, push the car through the sand to get it started, and then leave it running or we wouldn't get it started again. That meant we had to keep stopping for gas, though, and it wasn't very plentiful. At one point, the needle was on empty, and we still had 120 miles to go. Somehow we got there. On the way back, the terrible dirt roads and corrugated steel plates covering potholes created all sorts of vibrations in the car. We pulled into a fuel station, and the first pump was empty. So we pulled up to the next one, and the steering wheel just turned around and around. We crawled underneath the car and saw that the last of the little disks that make up the steering column had come out. We must have been losing the disks throughout our trip.

Why didn't the last one fall out when we were driving at high speeds or in the mountains? Why did it fall out right there at the gas station where we could get help?

Of course the station didn't have the parts, so the workers just got pieces of metal and cut new parts, filed them down, put them in the car, and sent us on our way.

These kinds of occurrences were standard. What used to annoy me as a young boy was that God didn't perform these miracles when I wanted Him to. He just seemed to have other priorities.

Jimmy was the first person buried in the little graveyard in back of our hospital.

Sometimes we tend to disregard the miracles God performs in situations where we think He's not active at all. That's what happened with my brother, Jimmy. He was a bright kid, but he got into a lot of trouble. I recently read a letter between my parents, and Dad said to Mother, "Yes, Jimmy is having some problems, but God assured me He has something very special for Jimmy."

Later, as they were driving to a council meeting, Jimmy complained of extreme pain. Mother recognized it as appendicitis, so they took him to the hospital, opened him up, and during the operation the appendix ruptured. There was no penicillin available. Jimmy died. He was the first person buried in the little graveyard in back of our hospital. There are many missionaries buried there now, including my mother.

People asked why this happened to Jimmy. But when I look at the letters my parents received and the people brought together through his death, I see that it had a powerful impact on the development of the Church of the Nazarene in Africa. It brought together a group of missionaries that had been in conflict with one another during a particularly stressful and pressured time. Shortly before he died, Jimmy testified to the saving grace of Jesus Christ, and Mother had just written to Dad, "Jimmy is a different boy."

I remember thinking this about him too. After he was saved, Jimmy was suddenly the peacekeeper when I got into fights with the neighbor kids. I once got into a wagon with some of the other kids, and we were fighting about who was going to pull it. I was arguing that the person who owned the wagon should be able to ride it and someone else should pull it. It was Jimmy's wagon, but I said it was mine. We were on the verge of a fistfight when Jimmy came up, grabbed the handle, and pulled us all around.

People from other parts of Africa wrote to my parents that Jimmy's transformation was an example of the faithfulness of God and an encouragement for them to keep giving their own painful struggles to the Lord.

The way God used this tragedy was a miracle.

God was at work. We forget sometimes that God performs more than miracles of healing; He performs miracles of transformation. And the greatest of all those miracles is when He let His own Son die for us. Jesus died, enabling our own transformation.

Sometimes we don't see the result of the miracles until years later. The best example I can think of is Lorraine Schultz, who was appointed principal of one of the Bible colleges in the 1950s. With her committee's approval, she added a course in secretarial work to the curriculum. She felt that no one knew how to do administrative tasks, and people needed training in bookkeeping, money matters, and so forth. That way they could teach people in their own churches how to do it.

Other missionaries thought she was crazy. They said, "These people are so poor—they can't afford to buy typewriters, so why teach them typing?" Lorraine felt a lot of pressure. It became worse when she opened that program because a lot of people in the community wanted to come to the Bible college to take both Bible and secretarial courses. It grew like wildfire. There were 35 to 40 students in the ministerial program and about 150 in the secretarial program.

Bible colleges in other parts of Africa said this practice wasn't fair because our school was getting money to run a Bible college and we were using it to run a secretarial school. They said we were running a school on false pretenses. It got very nasty and hurt Lorraine deeply.

In the 1970s, Lorraine had to leave Mozambique because of its civil war, and the Communists took over. They went throughout the country and drove out the Portuguese—especially the educated Portuguese. That meant all of the new Communist officials needed new secretaries for their offices, and the ones trained at the Bible college turned up everywhere. Those secretaries changed the minds of many of the leaders about the role of the church in the country, and that opened the door for us to go back into Mozambique even after the Communists had declared church illegal.

Those secretaries were powerfully used by God. I saw it firsthand when I went back to Mozambique to find a place for the Bible college to begin meeting again. Everywhere I went I talked with officials and their secretaries and discovered that the secretaries were members of the Church of the Nazarene and had been trained at the college.

Lorraine had no idea she would be helping redeem a country and keep God's work alive there. Churches were started throughout the country during the civil war through secretaries who had kept their Bibles and began conducting Bible studies in their homes. We received stunning letters from a pastor traveling throughout the country as a church planter, saying, "I organized five churches this week. We have 80 people in this one, 110 in that one." Every week he reported organizing four, five, and six more churches. Our church leaders thought maybe he had adopted a creative method of adding members, perhaps by taking a little bowl of water, sprinkling it on whoever was within reach, and saying, "You guys want to be Nazarenes? Here—you're Nazarenes." But when we looked into it, we saw that these were congregations that had been started by the secretaries who had been trained in our school years before. "I never said I started these churches," the church planter told us. "I just said I organized them. They were already there, already developing."

God wasn't leading trained pastors during the time of Communist rule; He was leading secretaries who loved God, who ended up starting churches all over Mozambique. This was one of the main reasons why we had a large explosion of churches opening up everywhere—and it came out of conflict. God took a divisive, ugly situation of vehement disagreement and did what needed to be done. We assume that holiness people aren't supposed to have conflict, and this one was covered up. But God used one stubborn woman who did what she thought was right despite the criticism she took.

The role of women in our work in Mozambique

progressed over the years. At first we didn't have many women pastors, but now we do. In fact, the largest church in Africa is pastored by a woman. This developed as the role of women has become increasingly recognized.

Used Candy Bars

People supporting us from the United States sent us gift packages every once in a while. But if anything new was sent, we had to pay a very expensive duty on it. As a result, we asked people to be careful with what they shipped to us. One day we received a box of Hershey candy bars. It was labeled "Used." Every single candy bar had a bite taken out of it. Then, in the bottom of the box, we found a bag with all the bitten off pieces, along with some false teeth with a note that said, "You said it had to be used."

We also received many shipments of cloth for us to make clothes. One day I noticed that no one in the congregation was wearing anything from a recent cloth shipment. I asked what happened to all of it, and the people said they had sent the cloth up into the villages where people didn't have enough clothes. They had caught the spirit of Christianity.

As I think about future generations serving as missionaries, I believe their commitment must not be to a church, like the Church of the Nazarene.

Their commitment must be to the Person of Jesus Christ. When we make that kind of commitment to Him, we do what He asks of us even if that changes from time to time or even creates a temporary conflict. You can't be a true missionary unless you are committed that way. I also don't think you can be a pastor without that kind of commitment. To be a true servant of God, we must be prepared to make the commitment that He is our all in all and allow His Spirit to take charge of our lives.

If we have the idea that God has chosen me, and now you're going to come and give your blessing to me, we've got it backward. We must come to serve. But if we're going to serve, we have to listen to what people need. And we can't just listen to their words—we have to listen to their lives, their hearts, to what's going on. Most of all, we must listen to God.

4 SOLD OUT IN SAGEBRUSH

by Kathy Mosteller Loeber

Kathy Mosteller Loeber is the oldest daughter of Earl and Gladys Mosteller. The Mostellers pioneered three areas of mission work for the Church of the Nazarene in Brazil, Portugal, and the Azores. They also worked in the Cape Verde Islands. Earl was a missionary until age 72, when he "technically" retired.

My dad's missionary career started when he was growing up in South Dakota. A schoolteacher sent him a postcard every week, 52 weeks out of the year, inviting him and his family to church. My dad's family was not interested in church at all. Finally my grandfather said they should go so this lady didn't spend all of her money on postcards. So everyone went to church, and that was Dad's introduction. I think his gift for evangelism might have been affected by this teacher's persistence.

At church Dad went to the altar frequently to pray because he couldn't get clarity on his relationship with the Lord. He had a great deal of uncertainty as to what God wanted him to do with his life. Then he went to Northwest Nazarene University (NNU) in Idaho.

Earl and Gladys Mosteller

My mom also attended NNU where she met my dad. She had become a Christian in her late teens and felt that perhaps God was leading her toward becoming a missionary. But Dad didn't want to get too involved with Mom because he didn't want his lack of clarity with God to interfere with her call to the mission field.

Mom made a commitment to God that she would fast and pray for Dad to become more solid in his spiritual life. Someone took a picture that I now have of my dad out in the sagebrush on his knees with his Bible. That's where he would go to pray. He didn't want to just be OK with God—he wanted to be completely sold out to Him. He wanted nothing obstructing God from becoming everything in his life. He did not sense a call to missions at this point, but he wanted to completely surrender to whatever it was that God had for him. He went to the altar at college many times and prayed out in the sagebrush for hours on end until there was nothing left to give God. He wanted his heart purified completely. He didn't settle for anything less than heart holiness.

Write to Kansas City

After they married, Mom and Dad served as pastors in a tiny church in Oregon for a while. They had their daily devotions both individually and together. They used to read *The Other Sheep* as part of their devotions, and Dad kept a diary of what he called "missionary incidents." Mom still felt called to missions but didn't know what to do with it since they were pastors in the United States. But in *The Other Sheep* they read that there was a strong need for missionaries. My mom started crying as she read the article, and my dad said, "Well, do you want me to enter this in the diary?" She replied, "If you're going to write anything down, write to Kansas City and tell them we'll be missionaries."

It was a moment of confirmation for Dad. He didn't receive a tremendous sign—just an assurance that this was the right thing to do. It was one more step in his persistent desire to follow God completely. As he kept saying out in the sagebrush, he didn't want just part of what God had in mind for him. He wanted everything. This was the sealing of his commitment. There was no turning back.

Confidence came along with this experience. Dad discovered that living at that level of the Spirit meant the decisions and plans and dreams and big thoughts God gave him were all part of God's plan. He had no doubt. For Dad it was full throttle ahead. That's how he lived.

I went to boarding school in the Alps of Brazil, many miles from home. It was a time of great spiritual growth, and I believed the Lord had a good thing in mind for me. Many of the kids cried a lot, and I often tucked them into bed, prayed with them, and told them Bible stories because they missed home so much. I thought to myself then, "Never will I put my kid through this." But I was already starting to grow up, and I had a spiritual grounding, so that helped me not to have a problem with being so far away.

Our church held prayer and fasting meetings at least once a week. This was very important to the work my father was doing. What made him happy was when he would stand back and see what the Lord was doing in a country. To see a country unfold before God, to see districts develop, to see the Lord do all this gave him joy beyond description. He also was very gifted in personal evangelism, which he practiced everywhere, on everyone, at any time.

An interesting thing to me is that even though my parents had this call to the mission field, they made it clear to my sisters and me that we had choices to make in our own lives. They always set aside time when we spoke English in the home, and they had us take correspondence courses so that we wouldn't be maladjusted when we returned to the United States on furloughs. But their attitude was that we had some freedom, and we didn't have to feel constrained or pressed to be part of the mission work. As a result, all three of us girls chose to be participants, not observers, in their work.

We were all strong-willed girls, and the latitude our parents gave us brought great joy to the work we were doing. It was not forced on us, but we bought into it and agreed 100 percent. We could see the purpose, the importance, and the vision, and we wanted to be part of it.

I never felt deprived growing up as a missionary's daughter. I didn't even like to go on furlough because Dad was gone all the time on his deputation schedule. Three of my grandparents died while we were on the mission field, and Mom and Dad were not able to return or even find out in a timely way. That was a difficult thing—to lose family members and not even be aware that they were gone. Still, I never heard anything negative from my parents, even behind closed doors. All I ever heard about was the privilege of doing what we were doing.

Healing

Since I grew up speaking Portuguese, I never had the language problem of getting certain words wrong. But one time my dad preached about Moses taking off his shoes because he was on holy ground, and in Portuguese shoes and pants sound alike. So there you go. He pretty much lost the service.

In Cape Verde we had only one surgeon for the nine islands, so you had to coincide getting ill with his visits.

My dad suffered terribly from malaria, even to where it was impeding his work. Then one day it just stopped. Much later, when he was in the United States, someone came up to him and asked, "Was anything going on at such and such time?" It was right during the time he was so ill and suddenly got better. The person said, "We got up in the night and prayed through for you." Who knew? God performed a miracle. These people didn't know that there had been an answer to their prayers, and Dad had no idea that someone had prayed.

That was one of the recurring lessons of life as a missionary family: We don't always need to know what God has done. We just need to know that His hand is moving on our behalf.

In Cape Verde we had only one surgeon for the nine islands, so you had to coincide getting ill with his visits. I was pretty sickly, and I needed my adenoids taken out. The surgeon wasn't planning on giving me any anesthetic, but my father intervened and insisted that the doctor give me something for the pain. Now, my dad passes out at the sight of blood. Finally the surgeon produced a gigantic needle and injected the local anesthetic into my nose. Then the doctor had to care for my father.

Because my parents had their daily devotions both personally and together, they received the strength and power to handle the adversities as well as the good things that came. Their foundation was having knowledge that God works everything for good and that we are in His hands.

Dad was given freedom and space to open new works. The people he worked with were all visionaries. They started Bible school correspondence courses and even built portable tabernacles that could be moved and reconstructed. Brazil asked for writings of Wylie and other Nazarene theologians. My parents translated them and put the writings in local newspapers before there were even any churches there. It was one of the methods God used to prepare an area for the arrival of a new Nazarene church.

The most important thing people can do to prepare for missions work is to have their relationship with God right. If you have sold out to God, then the call on your life will be there. But being sold out is first and foremost. Then you'll be able to recognize His voice, be in tune with it, and understand it. Many times the call to be a missionary can be for a specific time, just like God called Gideon and Samson for specific times. The Spirit of the Lord was on them for a particular time and a particular task, and then He released them. The issue of time spent for a missionary, whether it is 2 years or 10 or 45 or whatever, is all part of God's plan. But everyone has to go to the sagebrush of their lives to settle the question of who owns them once and for all.

5 SISTER SO-AND-SO'S CALL

by John Seaman

John Seaman's parents, Lauren and Nell Seaman, served as medical missionaries in Swaziland. John was born in Africa. He and his wife, Linda, served as missionaries in Martinique and in West Africa.

My dad was a disciplined person—even when he was young. Growing up, he knew two things: he wanted to become a doctor, and he wanted nothing to do with God. He was not interested in spiritual things, so he did not have one of those encounters with God calling him to be a missionary at a very young age. I've talked with people who knew him back then, and they said he was a kind of a problem kid because he was so disinterested in being a Christian. In fact, he was pugnacious about it.

Dad told me one of the reasons he resisted Christ was because he was afraid he wouldn't be able to be a doctor if he became a Christian. He went to Northwest Nazarene University in Idaho since it was close to home and because his parents had helped start the Nazarene work in Idaho. While he was a student, he attended a revival on campus, and it was one of those clean sweeps—except for my dad. He sat in the back with a look on his face that said, "Don't come near me." But the students kept praying, and finally Lauren Seaman got saved. All of a sudden that same discipline and tenacity and stubbornness was moved from the other side to helping him be everything God wanted him to be. He was fixed on that until the day he died.

Spiritual Malaise

Dad wrestled, though, with the issue of God's call. Once he had given his life to Christ, he wanted it to be all or nothing—100 percent. But he came from a family and a church that interpreted following God to mean he needed to become a pastor. They were well-meaning people, and Dad was very sensitive to them and wanted to do the right thing. He said, "Well, they know what they're talking about. They're godly men and women." So he abandoned his medical education for theological studies in preparation for the ministry.

As soon as he did that, a spiritual malaise took over. He wasn't happy; he wasn't joyful. He lost the thrill of it all, and his spiritual life became a struggle.

Finally it occurred to him, "Maybe God's not calling me to preach. Maybe Sister So-and-So is calling me to preach, but God isn't." He went back to his medical studies, and immediately the joy came back of serving Christ, of being a witness, and of studying theology and the Word. I think it's ironic that it took abandoning becoming a preacher to be able to love God's Word and theology again. But that's the way it was for Dad—he was fixed on serving God and realized that, in fact, *his* dream was also *God's* dream for his life.

God then began to bring a new dimension to his call. While studying the Bible, Dad was drawn to Psalm 96, verses 1-3: "Sing to the LORD a new song; sing to the LORD, all the earth. Sing to the LORD, praise his name; proclaim his salvation day after day. Declare his glory among the nations, his marvelous deeds among all peoples." These verses, as well as the parallel passage in 1 Chronicles 16 were significant to Dad because through them he sensed God calling him to missionary service, specifically medical missions. He also felt his degree in religion and philosophy from NNU was the best preparation he could have had to become a physician because it settled him intellectually for his medical studies. General superintendents also remarked that he was the finest layman theologian they had met.

The Church of the Nazarene had medical work in India and Swaziland at the time, both of which were still part of the British Empire. Dad knew that if a person had medical credentials from a school within the British Commonwealth, they were easily transferred and recognized within the Commonwealth. So he attended the University of Alberta, Canada.

Here was this young Nazarene guy, becoming a doctor, attending a church in Canada, with all sorts of women fluttering around him. The only person who attracted his attention, though, was Nell Gregory, who didn't give him the time of day. She had come to Canada from England with her family.

Eventually she did pay some attention to him, and she turned out to be a very strong woman. Now, my dad came out of a background that had a very narrow-minded view of things. In those days, members of the Church of the Nazarene weren't supposed to wear jewelry of any kind. He wanted to marry Nell Gregory, but he didn't feel that he could give her a wedding ring. So Nell said, "No wedding ring, no wedding."

He broke down and got her a wedding band. But other potential conflicts remained. He was called to be a medical missionary, and she was not. She was a very godly woman, but she never testified that she was called to missions. Still, she knew that God wanted her to be Lauren Seaman's wife. Her understanding was, "If that is what God wants, then God wants me to be a good missionary."

Mom and Dad married, then Dad completed medical school and practiced medicine in Canada as World War II raged on. When the church began

Lauren and Nell Seaman with their two daughters
before departing for Africa

sending missionaries again, my parents boarded a
boat headed for Africa, went around South America,
and landed in Argentina. It was still too dangerous

to cross the ocean. So my parents and two sisters stayed with Ray Hendrix's family for several months. My dad became very ill there, and it was providential he was able to be cared for in a modern hospital before going on to Swaziland.

Commitment

Our family moved back to the United States when I was about three due to some conflicts on the field. Back in Chicago, we opened our home to missionaries when they were in our part of the country, and I was constantly seeing people who never lost their focus. I think God used that constant exposure to these spiritual giants to help shape my own heart.

When God calls us, I believe He uses the environment we live in. Many of us who became missionaries grew up in homes of missionaries. And even though I didn't spend my entire childhood on the mission field, there was still something about my home that created an atmosphere for God to speak to me.

One of the more difficult issues my parents faced on the field had to do with educating their kids. While they had made a commitment that said, "Whatever it takes, we're going to obey," it sometimes meant painful separations and experiences. I've heard my family tell of the time they took Connie, my oldest sister, to boarding school. After they had said all of their good-byes and drove away, she stood behind the iron gate railing with her arms through it crying, "Mommy, don't go!"

My other sister, Betty, has very bitter memories about her boarding school experience. To this day she talks about it as being very negative and painful.

I think about that situation like this: my parents and grandparents had such a profound commitment to God and to His call on their lives that even though they didn't want to send their kids to boarding school, God called them to die to themselves—to sacrifice. As unpleasant as that might be, they also knew God cared about their kids going to school.

One of the differences I see between missionaries today and those of my parents' and grandparents' generations is that today we have some people looking at certain tasks or parts of the world and saying, "I won't do that—couldn't go there." I think it's important that we maintain a level of commitment that says, "God will provide; God will take care." That's the kind of spirit that affected me as a young person.

Sustained by the Call

The word "call" is often neglected today. It means that nothing will deviate us but God himself. At some points along my parents' careers, and in my own immediate family's careers, if we hadn't had the absolute certainty that God had called us to be missionaries, we would have been gone in a minute. Many times it would have been so easy to just do something else.

When Linda and I went to Martinique and tried to find a language teacher, we looked for nearly two years without success. We did everything we could to find a teacher. It was anguishing. I also know we were looked upon as incompetent, and that was troubling. If it hadn't been for the call, and my memory of those missionaries who faced far more difficult circumstances, we would have been gone in a hurry. I could have been pumping gas in Olathe, Kansas, and been more effective for God. But God had called us to be missionaries, and we couldn't get away from that. We had seen our parents and others wrestle similarly. It was this call that kept us focused and made us realize that we were just on the shelf in Martinique like this for a while—the rest was out of our control.

People called to missions have to assume, "I'm here forever, or until Jesus changes things."

When our daughter Kendra was severely injured in a car accident in the United States, doctors told us that she was either going to die or live in a vegetative state (thankfully, neither happened). People said to us, "Well, you have done your time overseas; come on home." They acted as if we were doing a prison sentence. That mystified us. Our missionary work meant everything to us, and it was our home. The call kept us going.

People called to missions have to assume, "I'm here forever, or until Jesus changes things." It can't be changed because things get inconvenient or because a person might think this would be a good thing to do for a while before he or she gets on with real life. The call is the fundamental issue.

For years I encountered a man whose vow was to run me out of Africa. Another person said terribly slanderous things to me that were so hateful it bordered on being physically abusive. Without God's call on my heart, my response would have been, "I don't need this. I don't need to have people telling lies about me and slandering my character. It's too painful." For the last few years we were in Abidjan in the Ivory Coast, we lived with mortar shells bursting in our neighborhood because of the civil war. Since we were white, we were suspected of being French, which put us in grave danger. So I worked hard on making my Chicago accent come through. They'd hear me speak and say, "This boy's definitely not from Paris!"

No one wants those kinds of stresses and pressures. But it was the call that kept us going through the hard times, just as we saw it sustain those who went before us.

Conflicts are everywhere. My parents had to live with conflict among sanctified people in the early work in Africa—wonderful people who loved God with all their hearts, and whose desire was to be everything God wanted them to be. And yet through vehement differences of opinion or philosophy, their character and call were tested severely. My mom and dad had to leave a missionary assignment that they didn't want to leave, but they did it with a spirit and attitude of Christlikeness.

I admire how the previous generations built up churches of solid people who know what it means to be sanctified through and through. They didn't rush through rapid church growth movements where the emphasis was on numbers. Instead they took the time to build a solid, mature leadership. The temptation is to criticize these generations for not having a great multiplication of growth. But if you look at the leadership in some of these places today—people who are from the soil of their own countries—you see them shepherding a viable church with a deep anchoring in God. This is from the investment of previous generations of missionaries.

If you look at the Portuguese-speaking world alone, you'll see this amazing effect at work. We don't have many Nazarene members in the Cape Verde Islands, but if you look at Brazil, the northeastern United States, the Azores, the Netherlands,

Portugal, France, and other places that have been affected by Cape Verdean migration, you'll see a profound impact. This illustrates the influence of those earlier missionaries who established the church across those islands—a place very few people in the world have even heard of. But that's the result of the patience and persistence and perseverance of those who worked so faithfully. The infiltration around the world is incredible.

This Is Home

In Africa, my parents did everything they could to make it our home. When I moved back there with Linda, my mom insisted that Linda take her beautiful English bone china with us. Linda was just going to put it in storage because it was so valuable and precious and expensive. But my mom sat Linda down and said, "You need to take this stuff. Who cares if there is a civil war and you lose it? It's just stuff." My parents helped us realize that we needed to make our time there special. They helped us create a home that our children loved.

At Christmastime people always wanted to see how Linda decorated the house. And when we were on furlough, our kids could hardly wait to get back to Abidjan, because it felt like home.

Some of my colleagues across the years, some from other mission groups, approached their assign-

Lauren and Nell Seaman in later years

ments as if they were camping out. Instead of saying, "This is forever. This is my home. This is where my heart is," they were saying, "This isn't home. This isn't permanent." They were also the ones who seemed the most unhappy.

We saw many miracles when I was growing up in Swaziland and when I went back to Africa as an adult. We tend to get excited about the startling, miraculous events because it's the kind of thing you can point to when you are defending the faith. But there are also the more mundane miracles where God grants the insights, the perceptions, or stimulates the mind to do something or probe further. For instance, in Swaziland my dad had to operate on my sister Connie when she was a little girl. While they had her opened up, Dad had the sense that they needed to look for something more. A heated debate went on among the medical folks surrounding that table, and he was told there was nothing else for them to do. But Dad said, "No, she's my daughter and I would like to look a little further." They probed more deeply and found a cancerous growth. She was only eight or nine, and back then it would have killed her.

Now why would my dad even think, "You know, while we've got the body open, let's go on a hike"? There's something to that—there's a sense of wisdom that comes along. Sometimes you just say the right word, and then you hear later, "Because your mom or dad said this, the direction of my life changed forever—it made me avoid a decision that would have been destructive." I think those are miracles.

On the flip side, I think we tend to overlook the evil in the world as well. We have a vulnerability in the western, or modern world. It is a blasé attitude that keeps our defenses down. In France, for instance, a country that declares itself more or less unbelieving in terms of God, they have the largest center for the occult in the whole world. The witches and warlocks greatly outnumber evangelical pastors in France. We cannot deny that there is a spiritual battle going on around the world.

On a lighter note, we have had some interesting experiences going back and forth between the modern world and the one where we served as missionaries. We weren't always ready for the changes in the culture that occurred in our absence. For example, when we left the United States for the Ivory Coast, there were no such things as megasupermarkets or wholesale stores.

After we had been gone a few years and came back to the United States on furlough, Linda asked me to go to the store to buy some potato chips. I jumped in the car and went into this new, gargantuan supermarket that didn't exist the last time I was in this country. I got the oversized cart and pushed it around toward where the chips might be. In Abidjan, we had one supermarket, and in good seasons we had two choices of potato chips. I was thinking along these lines when I arrived at the end of an aisle. As far as the eye could see, all the way down, on both sides, were chips of every kind. Chips light, flavored chips, rippled chips, and chips with the peeling still on the edges. Expensive and cheap chips. Unsalted and lots of salt chips. Sea salt chips. Did I mention the vinegar and oil chips? The ranch-dip chips sounded pretty good. I wondered how much worse the cheap chips tasted from the expensive chips. I didn't want to get a tasteless chip, but I didn't want to spend a lot of money.

I literally stood there, with my stomach churning. I was overwhelmed. Paralyzed. I finally just turned around and went home. I didn't buy chips that day.

Role Models

The role of women in ministry around the world is still developing. When I was growing up on the field, a missionary woman could have a role that the native ethnic woman could not. A missionary woman could teach at the Bible school. She might preach. But because of the cultural context of the women from the community, few local women had visible leadership roles. Everyone knew, however, that the village succeeded thanks to the women. The guys tended to sit around and be lazy, while the women were out in the fields, drawing the water, and making many of the real decisions. That double standard made the church structure issues a challenge, even though the Church of the Nazarene holds to a very strong position in terms of women and their roles theologically. The practical expression of those roles didn't always work into the local church, however.

The roles of missionaries in general are also still developing. I think the previous generations of missionaries had a different kind of responsibility than today's missionaries. Back then there was more primary evangelism, primary church growth, and pastoring. Now there is more of an emphasis on equipping the leadership and making sure the people are trained for the kind of work they need to be doing in their churches. In West Africa where I served, we had very small missionary teams spread out over a vast area, and not one was a pastor or had responsibilities similar to those who started the work. It's just not the same milieu for today's missionaries. So while we consider the great influence of these missionary heroes, what we really want is to take their commitment and their heart and their drive for God and for heart holiness and find ways to reshape it to the tasks and demands before us today.

When I think of those who have gone before us, I think they are the models of the kind of people we would like to be. In our moms and dads and grandparents we saw reflections of what Jesus is like in the flesh, in the context of their lives, in the good and the bad, the happy and the sad, the gain and the loss. Their lives continue to influence our lives.

Paul Orjala was my mentor. I was a student of his at the seminary. Whenever I was in a service where Paul Orjala was speaking, I would nearly go into cardiac arrest because of this great hero. I want to live up to what he would have thought was the right thing, and what my dad and mom, who are with the Lord, would think was the right thing. They have shown me the way.

CALL TO ACTION

After reading this book, please consider doing one or more of the following:

1. Pray for Nazarene missionaries serving around the world, that God will protect, guide, and sustain them.

2. Talk with your pastor or district NMI president about how your congregation can provide better support for your LINKS missionaries and other missionaries who might have special ties to your church.

3. Pray specifically for the children of missionaries, that the Lord will protect them and use their unique experiences to draw them closer to himself.

4. Find ways to "adopt" a missionary kid (MK) in college. Support him or her with prayer and small gifts throughout the year.

5. Pray for those who shared their stories in this book that God will continue to bless them and honor their faithfulness.

—Aimee Curtis, editor

PRONUNCIATION GUIDE

The following information will assist in pronouncing some unfamiliar words in this book. The suggested pronunciations, though not always precise, are close approximations of the way the terms are pronounced.

Azores	AY-zohrz
Birchard	BER-cherd
Cape Verde	CAYP VERD
Esselstyn	EHS-uhl-stuhn
Hynd	HIEND
Loeber	LOH-ber
Martinique	mahr-ten-EEK
Mosteller	MAHS-teh-ler
Orjala	ohr-YAH-lah
Schmelzenbach	SHMEHL-zuhn-bah